Jake an

in the
Mission to Mars

Written by Chris Bradford

Illustrated by Korky Paul

Collins

"Prepare for descent to the planet's surface," said Jen Jones, commander of the spaceship named Discovery.

Jake, science officer on the Mars mission, glanced at the visual display. "Our axis is wrong! Take emergency action!"

An explosion rocked the spaceship. "Autopilot failure!" Jake cried as they plunged downwards.

4

"Switch to manual control," Jen ordered. She piloted the shuttle's direction, but they were descending too fast.

Her knuckles went white as she wrestled with the controls. "Brace for impact!"

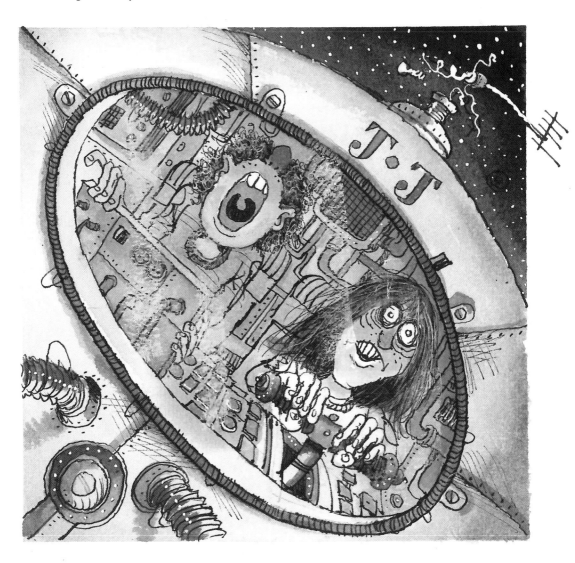

The ship bounced once then landed on an icy ridge.

6

"Nice flying, commander!" said Jake.

Jake and Jen put on their spacesuits. Jen checked her laser device. "Our instructions are to collect unusual rocks and look for evidence of life," she explained.

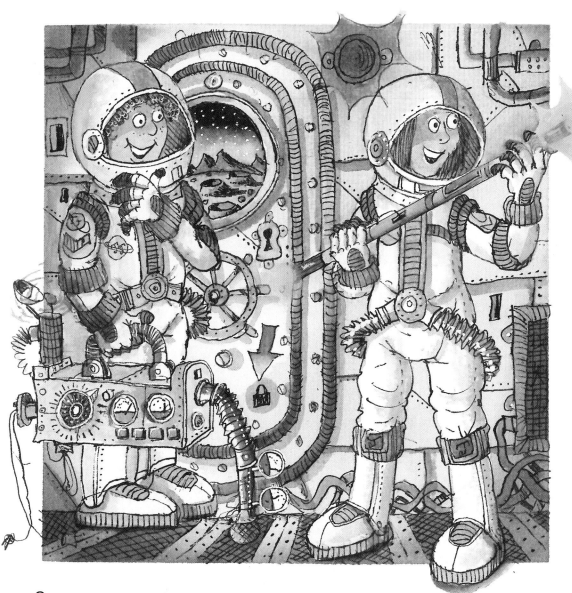

Climbing down to the surface, Jake took measurements.
"There's little atmosphere," he noted. "To ensure we limit exposure from cosmic rays, we must be quick."

As they investigated the planet's red rocky surface, Jen bounced high into the air. "I feel almost weightless!"

Jake knew why. "Gravity on Mars is about sixty percent less than on Earth."

From high up, Jen noticed an unusual glow. She led Jake to its location behind the ridge.

Jake bent down on one knee to get a closer look. "This is a very strange piece of rock. It's opaque yet glows inside!"

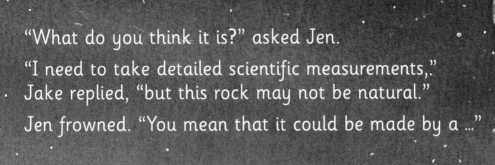

"What do you think it is?" asked Jen.

"I need to take detailed scientific measurements," Jake replied, "but this rock may not be natural."

Jen frowned. "You mean that it could be made by a …"

13

'MARTIAN!' screamed Jake, falling backwards against a rock.

The creature was the size of a garden gnome with eight octopus-like arms and four crescent-shaped eyes that glittered like sugar lumps.

Startled, Jake and Jen raced back towards their spaceship. But there was a rip in Jake's spacesuit.

"I'm running out of oxygen," gasped Jake. "My limbs are going numb!"

Jen wrapped her arms around Jake. With less gravity she could support his weight and she helped him in the direction of the ship's airlock.

But as they ascended the icy ridge, another terrifying Martian pounced on them.

This one was larger and hideous. With green wrinkly skin and no limbs at all, it looked like a huge slug. Rising up, the Martian gnashed its teeth and let out a moan.

Jen dazzled it with her laser. Blinded, the Martian writhed in pain and tumbled off the edge. Jake and Jen dived into the safety of their spaceship.

Peering out of the tent's "airlock", Jake and Jen sniggered as their older brother stumbled around the campsite in the darkness. Wrapped in his sleeping bag, Shane tripped over a rope and fell onto his face.

"That sure is one monstrous Martian!" giggled Jake.

"But if our brother is the slug, who was the first creature?" asked Jen.

Glancing up, Jake spotted a shooting star racing across the night sky. He stared at Jen, numb with shock. "Do you think we had a real close encounter with a Martian?"

After reading

Letters and Sounds: Phase 5–6

Word count: 500

Focus phonemes: /n/ kn, gn /m/ mb /r/ wr /s/ c, ce, sc /c/ qu, x /zh/ s /sh/ ti, si, ssi, s

Common exception words: of, to, the, into, are, said, do, were, one, once, our, their, who, eyes

Curriculum links: Science; PSHE

National Curriculum learning objectives: Reading/word reading: apply phonic knowledge and skills as the route to decode words; read common exception words, noting unusual correspondences between spelling and sound and where these occur in the word; read other words of more than one syllable that contain taught GPCs; Reading/comprehension: develop pleasure in reading, motivation to read, vocabulary and understanding by being encouraged to link what they read or hear to their own experiences

Developing fluency

- Your child may enjoy hearing you read the book.
- Take turns to read a page of the main text, encouraging the use of different voices for each character.

Phonic practice

- Challenge your child to identify the /sh/ or /zh/ sounds in each of these words: unusual, mission, measurements, visual, direction
- Challenge them to think of other /sh/ words ending in -ssion and -tion. (e.g. *possession, passion; action, instruction*)

Extending vocabulary

- Point to the word **investigated** on page 10 and challenge your child to suggest a synonym. (e.g. *examined, analysed*) Focusing on verbs, repeat for **noticed** on page 11. (e.g. *spotted, saw*)
- Take turns to point to a verb and challenge each other to suggest a synonym.

Comprehension

- Turn to pages 22 and 23. Point to the spaceship on page 22, and then identify the tent on bottom left of page 23 as being the children's "spaceship". Using the two maps as prompts, ask your child to match the events on the imagined mission with places and things in the campsite.